DIARY OF A CELL

Diary of a Cell

Jennifer Gresham

STEEL TOE BOOKS • BOWLING GREEN

Cover and book design by Scott Poole

First Edition
Steel Toe Books
English Department
20C Cherry Hall
Western Kentucky University
1 Big Red Way
Bowling Green, KY 42101-3576

ISBN: 0-9743264-1-0

In memory of my parents,
and for my husband, Kyle

CONTENTS

III

IV

At a time when Math and Science not only regulate, but create large portions of the human environment—when to be ignorant of those two fields is to fundamentaly misperceive the world—too many poets either mimic 19th-century pastoralists, kowtow to pseudo-scientific literary-political theorists, or parrot a few terms (uncertainty, relativity, unified field . . .), and believe themselves versifying Einsteins. Plenty of poets can generate impressive-sounding verbiage; not so many can actually—with scientific rigor, imagination, and clarity—think. Jennifer Gresham is a poet who can.

Like current literary studies, science thrives on theories and wild speculation; unlike those studies, science requires verifiable evidence. Even when it approaches the limits of our ability to perceive and comprehend, it is intent on uncovering Truth—or as close to Truth as it can get. Science is, as it's etymology suggests, a way to know the world: the best way we currently have. Since the world is well worth knowing, I was delighted to choose Gresham's *Diary of a Cell* as winner of the 2004 Steel Toe Books Prize in Poetry. *Diary of a Cell* is full of poems that speak of science with a familiarity born of close association. Better yet, these poems speak of life with the deep understanding and reverence which science can give.

When Gresham writes "A Brief History of Mathematics," the reader learns quickly that for her, mathematics is more than a trope. When she speaks of "The Genius," we sense she's known a few. Even when she writes "The Mythology of Woman," she expresses the spirit of imaginative inquiry that fueled the ancients as, without the tools and methods of modern science, they tried to know their world.

Full of accurate analogies and well-drawn parallels, *Diary of a Cell* is an intelligent book—we expect that from a scientist; but it is more. It's lyrical ("At dusk, we retreat the way / we came, following the tributaries / of cement to suburbs like an undertow . . ."). It's passionate ("You hated him every time / he raised his hand, / for the way teachers / knit his words into lace . . . "). It's tender (". . . why the memory of kindness / can find us in the dark . . . "). It's brutal, and scathing ("I will miss everything / about your hard body / except the back of your hand . . . "). It's funny ("Scientists are like beetles / Crawling over the earth, antennae twitching . . ."). Above all, though, *Diary of a Cell* is poetic—not in a namby-pamby, sensitive-soul-in-an-insensitive-world way; in the strong and competent sense of poietes: maker.

This is just to say that Jennifer Gresham's book is eminently human. And humane. And a great pleasure: the kind students of Humanities need to know first-hand; the kind science tells us we human animals evolved to move toward, and to enjoy.

Charles Harper Webb
Final Judge
2004 Steel Toe Books Prize in Poetry

I

MY MOTHER WEARS A NEGLIGEE

In this picture, she is cupped
by light, clothed in something
like rain. The tree fuzzy
behind her, nipples steal
the foreground. She is aroused
by London, she is young.
In this picture, she is still
in love. Although she cannot see
it, I am there too, right below
the narrow of her waist,
where sunlight breaks
through the windowpane.
I am the tiny prism spilling
color from her womb, tumbling
headlong toward the camera
and my father's dark eye.

A buzz of excitement—carpenter bees
mate mid-flight in a twisted, golden ring.
Pear blossoms throw their soft white petals
into the street; even the morning light is hazy
with pollen. The Robins and the Orioles
flew in just for this occasion, small leaves
peek from behind branches for a better view.
And here I am, dreamy and dressed in ivory
linen, daffodils swaying expectantly behind me
like ladies in waiting, while wind chimes
flutter with the news. Giddy, I step
into the hushed aisle of the morning, accept
the proffered hand of Spring.

THE MACROECONOMICS OF BIRDS

Birds have no songs
for times of plenty, busily reaping
the rewards of yet another plague.
Not that they could be heard anyway,
above the rattle and sizzle
of insect bat mitzvahs.

The birds are getting fat.
One falls from his wire perch
above the highway straight into
the hand of gravity. He can't get up,
and sooner or later, a passing car
will absolve him of his gluttony.
But in this brief moment of flapping,
between the frenzied flutter of useless
wings, he calls out the one word
he learned when young: *more*.

We open our mouths,
hesitant,
wait for fish to rise
to the surface, the first
lilt of gold spawning
another sentence
until the words are river
and fish together, until
the sunrise is captured
in the reflection.

The teacher barely moves
her lips, hummingbirds
hidden in her mouth.
Drunk on the nectar
of language, sweet hum
of conversation, we don't care
what it means anymore;
Your pencil is ugly
almost a waterfall.

BODY OF WATER

The human body
is eighty percent water,
more miracle puddle
than anything else and
not immune to the laws
of ebb and flow. If the moon
can move oceans, why not us?
It is why we flood into cities
by day, flow down crowded streets
past other bodies, fill tall glass
buildings to do our work.
At dusk, we retreat the way
we came, following the tributaries
of cement to suburbs like an undertow,
Atlantis deserted once again.

It is why so many of us lead lives
that seem to go nowhere,
to lose all the ground we've gained;
why we never recognize
our own thirst or the depth
of our longing.

EMPTY CALORIES

You take away the after-dinner
chocolate, click your tongue
while pouring my coffee

down the drain. Instead of popcorn
during movies, you point suggestively
to a bowl of apples. I can't stop staring

at your mouth, remembering the days
you believed we could subsist
on love alone.

It began simply enough:
the need to count fish
or huts in the village.
How awkward the beginnings,
proofs always involving
a stack of mackerel
starting to collect flies
while the wisest men
counted and recounted
until they all could agree:
twelve fish.

The number zero came
later, discussed by
theologians staring into
the dark night. Deemed
dangerous, the number
was sequestered in a tall
tower for many years,
lest the people began

to wonder: *What if this
is all there is?* a logical
if-then statement even
the clergy could follow.

It was war that rescued
the number, made
nothing hard to ignore.
When a village was razed
to the ground and all
that remained was a great
circle of ash, a general
might ask, *How many
remain?* Zero.

Negative numbers quickly
followed the concept
of loss. A village razed
was more than nothing,
it became a scar on its
people, a vengeance
to be exacted. These
were the Dark Ages,

when people counted
backwards to tell
the story of their lives.

The Renaissance ushered
the imaginary numbers,
the ones you counted
in shifting clouds before
a storm, or in the soft
mumblings of a boy lost
to sleep. But this, like
so much, was fleeting.

And that brings us
to the present Age of
the Complex, numbers
built like a steam train,
an imaginary man waving
good-bye from inside
the cab as they pull away
from the station, and you,
just like in the old movies,
frantically chasing after,
wanting to follow.

THE GENIUS

You hated him every time
he raised his hand,
for the way teachers
knit his words into lace.
You resented how he watched
you struggle, brilliant machinations
hidden behind the gate
of his blank face.

But now, through his glass office,
you see how he broods,
counting the minutes and hours
since his last, great idea,
the time remaining
to solve the vast unsolved.
He leaves work at night
with shoulders slumped
as if carrying a large, invisible pack
filled with all the candles
he could not light.

Birthdays are the worst—
the clear trajectory of decline,
the sum of all the years
wasted: equations sunk,
one variable stuck in the cement
of his slowing mind, theories
softening like rotting meat.

Now, when he calls your attempts
amateur, you know he really means
I fear my best ideas are behind me,
and when he trumpets his own genius,
pity rises in you like a pale moon,
you, who never even tried
to eclipse the sun.

HOW MY PARENTS MET

California called you
as you slipped your sullen feet
into the pink hand-me-down
for prom, posed for a picture
against the white-washed wall
that embraced your slender shoulders.
Beyond grandfather's camera, your date
stamped his impatience like a horse,
the twang of his red hair impervious
to its curl, his teeth rotting
just a little more than yours

enough to make you swear off
country hicks forever, leave
for the frothy shores of Long Beach
where my father was waiting
to unpin the tight curls of your hair,
flash a quick smile like money.
He took you into his apartment
and with the skill of an alchemist

drained the drawl from your pores,
fired your skin until brown and crisp,
painted your teeth with promises
until they gleamed, until you were perfect:
silent and obedient and afraid
to leave, dependent upon the magician
who made the girl from North Carolina
disappear.

LOOKING FOR PHILLIP LEE

He might have become a governor
or garbage collector, for all my grandmother cared.
Or if he resembled my other uncles,
he might be on his third, fourth wife;
he might keep a gun under his pillow.

Instead, Phillip Lee was born a fish,
small gill whistling at the base of his spine,
gasping for the salty water
of my grandmother's womb.
And after the pneumonia
seized his tiny lungs forever,
he became the dark flash of dreams
unfulfilled, the son who could never be
called home. He became a hunger,
his bones became an old woman's last wish.

What will distinguish the matchsticks
of an uncle? Back in '33, Vegas
was a desert town, full of sage and wind.

His stone may no longer be readable.
His coffin, small as a cigar box,
may hide beneath a shiny slot machine
or water fountain wonder. *I hung a locket
around his neck*, she tells me, *that's how
you'll know it's him*, as if he was the only boy
to steal his mother's golden, gifted heart.

We would like to thank you
for the poems you sent
via carrier pigeon. Many,
including the title piece
(Life on a Deserted Island?)
did not survive the monsoon
of travel. Furthermore,
the pieces were not received
during our reading period.
We are including a copy
of our submission guidelines
for your convenience.

We were particularly interested
in the poem "Palm Fronds:
Breakfast, Lunch, & Dinner"
but felt it was a tad
hopeless in its conclusion.
Had you read a sample copy
you might know we prefer
uplifting, inspirational verse.

The pigeon, whom we nicknamed
Poopsy, claims he doesn't
remember the way home.
Normally, all such submissions
without a SASE are recycled
in the birdcage, but we think you
show great promise. So we decided
to enclose this letter in the drained bottle
of our favorite Merlot, intending
to drop it in the Pacific Ocean.
However, due to lack of funding,
we settled for a nearby pond,
with the hope it reaches you
in a timely fashion. Thanks
for the pigeon and your patience.

Warmly,
The Editors

II

Some children might have been too frightened
to ask, content to chase crickets
deep into the grass. But I begged.
In that dimming summer light
while we grilled steaks for dinner,
he transformed. His chest filled with air
like a sail at sea, tongs became
his sword, right hand raised high in oratory.
"Speak! Speak! thou fearful guest!"
Words boomed across the small backyard,
reciting his poem to the rhythm
of the dog's whine.

A faint accent trickled into his voice,
rendered fat dripped like pale blood
down his meaty arm. And for the length
of Longfellow's tale, I forgot
about his eyes, dark and dull
when he drank, how he sometimes
gripped my wrist too tight, too long.

When he stood there by the smoking grill,
he became a Viking of old; our house
and all its skeletons became eclipsed.

From tombstones, hands reach up
to wave, ripple like a series
of threadbare capes. His gas lawnmower
snorting, John charges and fingers fly—
a metacarpal chinks off the granite,
sinks into shade.

It's here at the Young Wood Cemetery
he feels most alive, never
has to worry if his laugh lingers
too long. Bill Parsons still grips
the shadow of his great bowl
of a belly, and Old Man Larson,
who made it to 91, reaches for his shoulder—
Hellava job, John—more greetings
than he ever could answer, and the children
(so many children!) scream his name,
Over here, John, over here
hollow sockets almost bright with
anticipation: *Legs up!* he tells them,

that old game he used to play
with Mother when she lugged the Hoover
through their small living room.

And now that his meds
have been peeled away like
layers of thick, sterile batting
that keep out most light and sound
and touch, everything reminds him of a family
picnic full of sunshine, grass freshly cut
down to the nub, where everyone
is lovely and he is the star;
where anything can be undone,
and it's no shame to have
a foot in the grave.

ANOREXIA

I've always been thin—
my body a machine
that likes to run, hear
the hum of its molecular
motors, the breakdown
of glucose a perfect
piston fire.

Some bodies
are anti-
technology,
strive for the
simplicity
of a single
blade of grass,
a piece of
scrim-shaw
whittled by
their own
fingers.

They embrace
feng-shui
to extreme:
see themselves
as the only
orchid in a
crowded room,
forgetting
even flowers
must grow
to bloom.

THE HEART PROCTORS ITS OWN EXAM

The brain offered to play
big brother, to take the boy
on a long walk, ask a series
of questions that would leave him
groveling or running
for his mother. A test, of sorts,
in the subjects of devotion,
faith, fitness, elocution,
heroics, humility—

the heart stopped
the list before it got too long.
No no no no no no no
It pounded the walls, demanded
to be treated like an adult.
I can do this myself, it claimed,
and proceeded to ask the boy
in for tea. It read his leaves,
longingly traced his palm.

The brain asked questions
in between sips. *Did he have*
a job? Did he know the number
of the local florist? But the heart
didn't care. It measured the clasp
of his hand, the curve of his lip.
Could he fix a car? Would he change
a diaper? The heart would walk,
the heart would do everything.

The brain sighed and tried to show
the boy the door. The plan backfired.
Now they were coming in,
all giggles, crossing the threshold
and walking boldly to chambers
that could never hold them.

and I have lined up
answering machine
cell phone, pager
like a set of suspects
and despite my fury,
still they plead
we know nothing
we know nothing.

I stand watch
before the front window,
hands curled tightly
behind my back; I curse
each pair of feet to pass
before me that do not belong
to you. Every distant siren
becomes the wail
of a new widow.

A woman knows for certain
when her man is in trouble.
It is you who are ignorant,
arriving suddenly with
an easy smile, flowers in hand.

DEAR STARFISH

You'll be happy to know
everything worked out just fine.
He explained

how another woman sometimes appears
a bright, shiny hook,
and he's just
a big, dumb fish, after all.

So he bit.

Boy, has he learned his lesson!
His mouth still hurts. Everything was dark.
He could hardly breathe
from shame. He told me he was *sorry*.

Now, he wants nothing more
than to explore the shallow depths
of monogamy

with me. I nearly stayed
where he put me, like a pretty,
hollow shell upon the shelf. But then
I thought of you, dear starfish, languid
and limp on the shore, how hard
it must be to watch the ocean
slink away.

PHOSPHORESCENCE

In the middle of the Indian Ocean
blue-green algae amasses

in glowing colonies, large
enough to make you nervous,

their phosphorescence not
the cryptic language you assume,

but simply the emission
of some earlier light—

the way a compliment can make you
become that person described,

why the memory of kindness
can find us in the dark.

Schrodinger knew about yearning,
had felt the same tug, been pulled
inexorably toward the nucleus
of his attraction. He was
a small, insignificant electron
in orbit around her. The path
between them, he found,
was predictable: his offerings
overshooting the boundaries
of acceptable, his disposition
lovesick and despicable.
Leave her uncertain
of your intentions, Heisenberg
advised. But it was no use.
He was charged, cursed,
circling her house at night,
despondent at the burning candles
calling him through the glass,
his inability to enter.

And so he wrote their story
in the devoted language

of his distance, describing
equations as waves, the sinusoidal
joy and repulsion she offered.
If only there were another solution,
to alter variables in his favor, ignore
the geometry of his position.
He ran the numbers again and again,
refusing to believe.

No one's told the crickets
here in this oasis of evening
where the house still outstretches
the sun, it's late morning.
So they sing:
high-pitched, drunken,
rhythmic voices reach
another crescendo, another rousing chorus
of Row, Row, Row Your Boat—
mugs empty, throats a little dry.

No one's told them this shade
is artifice: elsewhere their brothers
have curled into tiny grass beds, dream
about the prophecies of fireflies,
the horrors of lawn-mowers.
It's a dicey life, here
in the still dew-damp, south
side of the lawn. But
everyone's singing, their voices

calling merrily, merrily, merrily:
this darkness but a dream.

Zeus, god of storm and frustrated artist,
sculpted his figures from mist,
proverbial rib of cloud.

With wind as his chisel, creatures
formed and fell from the sky: frog,
bison, bird; figments of themselves
to populate the green earth.

But what he wanted was woman,
even if ephemeral, some company
in that isolated expanse of atmosphere.
By his hand, a mass of moisture swirled,
became an anvil, bed of creation.
Eager, he threw himself into his work,
each forceful breath bringing flashes
of exertion which streaked like veins
across the dark sky.

The mammatus formed first, a pendulous

shadow of flesh, nipple extended.
The funnel continued, touched down
with hips writhing, gyrating
to her own sweet whistle.
But what's born of desperation
is never easily controlled,
and like those that followed,
she uprooted all who tried to tame her.

SUBMERGED

The boy treads a path
to the river, ready to drown
the cat struggling in his pack,
its claws seeking his skin
through the dense fabric.
The pet might as well be
the girl who spurned him
herself.

He imagines how he will
clutch the cat by its cowl,
its fur filling his fist like
her dark locks, her eyes
splayed wide as lily pads
in fear.

The river is choked
with weeds, thick stalks
rising almost to his chest,
their heads swollen with seed
and, like him, ready to blow.

I scribbled my name
in rose water above the dark,
solid line, dotted my i
with a tiny heart
only you could see. I sent
the papers with a man big enough
to give them to you.

My Daddy always called me
passive   aggressive
when I filled his shoes with honey.

Please take this little survey:
Were your needs met?
Is your stomach really stone?
Can I have the china?

I will miss everything
about your hard body
except the back of your hand.

But yes: the opiate eyes,
chalk white of your smile,
the musk of your hide.

Now, now, don't be so glum.
I always thought of you
like a horseshoe in the grass
lucky   lucky   lucky
just a bit far from the pin.

It's the end of summer
and the flowers are packing up
their bags. I'm going with them.
My darling, I always wanted you
to be the first one served.

when i could not calculate
the waitress' tip, my lip
quavering under my Father's hard stare,
we began the summer of fractions:
dividing ourselves again and again,
the common denominator always
my Father: immutable, indivisible,
larger than ourselves, like a country
we pledged our lives to.

we drilled as soldiers:
3 by 4, 9 by 12
the pie in thirds, apples in eighths
always the same
long hours filled with
small numbers, the cadence
of decimals marching
filling my ears.

outside, the sound of children
playing cops and robbers,
cowboys and indians. where will you
draw the line, mother would ask?
and then it was clear
he would divide our resistance
piecemeal with his silence
until we were small, then smaller
zeros parading as the King's crown jewels.

III

What ever happened
to that imaginary friend
of yours? my mother asks
over Sunday brunch, as if
inquiring about an old
boyfriend or third cousin.

And I wonder myself exactly
when I stopped holding her hand
on the way to school, when
the closet contained only clothes?
How strange I shouldn't
remember the day,
the hour, she disappeared
as if someone had asked
When did your sister die?
and my only available reply—
I don't know.

One thing I know for certain:
there was no fight,

no messy, childhood divorce.
We simply went our separate ways,
quietly seeking companions
more like ourselves. I'd stay
late after school, she'd
skip class. Once I caught her
smoking under an oak
on the playground, a sly smile,
a quick elbow to the ribs.

After that, who knows?
She went the way of all
wild women, I suppose,
no time for postcards, tales
of a life I relinquished.

Imagine, if you will, three mice.
Contrary to what you have
heard, they are not blind
but are in a spaceship
traveling near the speed of light.
This makes them unavailable
for your supper, yes.

So these mice, traveling near
the speed of light, appear
quite fat, though there is
no cheese aboard. This is
simply a distortion of mass,
because the mass of a mouse
is nothing more than a bundle
of light, and vice versa. I see
how this might imply mice
are in the light fixtures,
undoubtedly a problem, so

let me try again.
If two people attempted
to feed you simultaneously,
no doubt a good situation,
but you were on a train
traveling near the speed
of light, the food would
appear unappetizing, falling
to the plate in slow motion,
an extended glob of protein
that never smelled good,
if you ask me, train or no.
The affinity of the food
for the plate, what we call
gravity, is really just
a stretch in the fabric
of a space-time continuum,
what happens when you
have sat in a seat too long,
perhaps on this very train.

Oh kitty, I know how you hate
to travel and the journey must
have made you tired. Come now,
lick your coat one more time

and let us make haste
from this strange city
of light and fantastic dream.

I remember that stiff
wooden chair, its own
form of torture, the
kidney shaped desk
curved about you like
pillory, the slow moving
clock (always in sight)
paced like a guard with
a cold heart and an eye
for detail. I doodled in
the margins of my thick,
spiral bound notebook
to ease my suffering,
while someone with more
guts had their hand
raised, an emissary from
the prison yard, insistent,
bouncing in that hard
seat, waiting for the teacher
to turn from the black-

board, from some equation
or timeline of battles, this
kid had just one question,
his hand rising like a
small balloon across the
blue sky of freedom,
a symbol of the solitary
answer we were all
burning to know.

THE ELEMENT REFUGEES

In addition to the hundred-odd names of existing elements, there were at least twice that number for elements that never made it, elements imagined or claimed to exist, but later found to be known elements or mixtures. —Oliver Sacks

Gone are the days of Moldavium.
Albamine slipped through the cracks,
and Virginium died a beggar's death.

Cast off their squares, stripped
of electrons, the element refugees
were exiled to the Diagram of the Forgotten,
the tenth circle of Hell, given
endless, blank space on which to build,
but banned from the table.

Some took it hard. Norwegium
had to be lured by blonde beauties,
then bound and gagged. Cassiopeium
sat down in her chair and refused to move.
Bohemium opened a small co-op,
taught the others to farm the land,
but never quite forgot the power of ownership.

As the myth goes, Panchromium tried
to convince the tabled gentry to keep him.
How many words are there for light?
he asked. *We can all coexist here.*
But Vanadium had already hung
her diplomas on the wall, begun
a pot of coffee. *But how many ways
can you say science?* She smiled.
Just one.

He was as entranced with the perfect helix
of her hair as he was with the tectonics
of her breast. He adored how she flushed
each time he said *parasympathetic*.

She was the lemon, he the copper wire.

The days he circled in lonely orbits
around girls as beautiful and terrible
as black holes now seemed like a dream,
one he could dissect with pushpin
labels: the heart of ridicule, empty stomach
of Friday nights, the squiggly entrails
of disappointment. Something learned
and now stored away, allowing him to transcend
the normal laws of high school, to distill
something pure.

In third grade science we learned about weather:
how hail, like gemstones, can be classified
by weight, how tidal waves can flood
your top-floor apartment with fish.

Before Mrs. Adams could begin her lesson
on lightning rods, I stood with all the authority
of a child whose father had graduated
from Naval Electronics School.
I explained how lightning begins from below,
pressure building among gloomy electrons
who wander aimlessly through the dark alleyways
beneath the Earth. But the lucky ones
find their way to the rod, climb its long spiral staircase
to the top, where the wind blows them off,
allowing them one last wish before dispersing.

When Mrs. Adams stopped me to make clear
that the rods don't prevent lightning,
but channel it, I suggested maybe she should

go back to school, which earned me my first trip
to the Principal's office.

Years later, after my father died,
I stood in his musty office, sobbed
to discover he was a fake:
my father the reverend, my father the M.D.,
the Naval engineer—all the documents doctored
by some hokey, mail-away place.
I climbed onto the roof, raised my fist
towards the heavens and scattered
the certificates to the wind, like wishes.

I pitched the driftwood back into the bay.
It clung to shore; refused to leave the cusp
of what it once called home. Even the roll
of salt and tide cannot remove a yearning.

What ties us to this place, makes us draw back
in search of calm? Instinct, perhaps, or else
a weariness that leaches bone. Time steals
our wish for something more than this. When I

hurl stones as far as they will go, ripples
race back to find me. All that I try to lose
returns. My body reaches out to grasp
the child my mind will not allow.

CLONE

What makes us imagine our clone
fully grown, a twin of bad habits,
worn-out dreams? We forget the clones
don't just *arrive*, as if from some back door
or magic mirror, but come, as we do,
from cells: beautiful, dividing sacks
of water and code.

What a golden opportunity to raise
yourself right! You'd teach yourself
Spanish early, smile at yourself
so much more than your parents did
and only be encouraging. You'd know
what's ahead. "Don't steal from the paper boy,"
you'd tell yourself, "you'll only regret it later."

No one likes a meddler. The clone
will feel smothered, second guessed.
*I can't take another day
of your harping*, she'll scrawl,
the handwriting so familiar,

ink of her own name barely dry
before she dashes through the giant door
of the world you carved her.

MY BODY SUFFERS A CIVIL WAR

In retrospect, it's obvious those scuffles
between left and right only built
bitter resentment, a feeling
one would have to go.

But as a kid, I was always one
for the underdog, and being right-handed,
like almost everyone else, I felt sorry
for the left. Why do you think they call it
left out? So I'd send my hands
into battle, one putting the other
in a choke hold, fingers curled about fingers,
rings biting into bone. And the left,
with its God-like champion, always won,
encircling the right until pliant, ready to give.

Now I see the error of my ways.
As I grew older, I forgot their petty
wars for dominance; no more fixed fights.
So when the lump appeared in my left
breast, I knew just who to blame.

BOOGER

You yank your nephew's finger from his nose,
his little arm straining against the injustice.
I'm digging, he explains, *I almost had it.*
He's miffed. You tell him it's gross, to use
a tissue, for God's sake, he knows better.
Instead he's sulking, waiting for a distraction.
And although you shoot him a look that says
Don't let me catch that nail by your nostril again,
the truth is you understand all too well,
better than you care to admit, the frustration:
after picking your way carefully through the dark,
after almost owning what you seek, you have to turn away.

DIARY OF A CELL

So much is the same:
small, easy to hide
in some cranny of the nucleus
or mitochondria, away from
scientists' prying eyes.
And always written in code;
a whole library of nothing more
than four letters strung together,
a tongue twister even if
you know the language.

Even the stories begin
with the familiar: proteins
saying good-bye at the cusp
of the membrane door, one
getting into his sub-cellular
compact, the other already fussing
in the cytoplasm, devising the next
meal. What's missing is the emotion.
Life, in its most intricate detail,

is beautiful in its routine. No sentiment,
no longing stare out the window.
It's all business here: the details
of their travel, where they are going,
the strange names of streets.

A LETTER FROM MRS. MUIR

When one tugs at a single thing in Nature, he finds it hitched to the rest
of the Universe. –John Muir

I must have searched
the yard a hundred times
before I found it, the secret
you said would be there.
I would have missed it
again had I not, in a moment
of industry, stopped to pull
a weed from the garden.

The cavern of soil
was filled with wild
creatures, blinded earwigs,
centipedes scurrying from
my hands. Digging deeper,
I found the things we thought
we'd lost: our discarded,
disjointed dreams, the swelling
lump from my breast, our

daughter, stoned and frightened,
ready to come home.

Deeper still, as you well
know, were the things
I never knew I had:
the kind thoughts of
strangers, a renewed
vigor, something to say
to the dead.

MOVIE STAR NAME

If you take your mother's first name
paired with the street
of your childhood home,
you become a star.
Say the name twice, whisper
Maggie Bay, Maggie Bay
and the surf becomes applause,
great cymbal clash of your debut.

Hurricane Elena sits on the
coastline as sea water begins
to lap the side of the house.
Fiddler crabs dance along
the edge of the pool, punching
their claws high into the humid air.
The houses, built on stilts,
sway as if swooning.

You close your eyes, say
your movie star name

again and again
until the wet, warm air rushes
to greet you like the tug
of a thousand hands, the flash
of bulbs burning behind
your lids. You say your name
until the soft, red carpet
of acclaim rolls beneath your feet
like water, until you're floating
in the world's embrace.

INHERITANCE

A 20-acre plot of Florida palmetto
waits patiently for my acceptance.
At night, iridescent green beetles
crawl the brush, ticking out messages in code.
I believe it says, quite simply, "Claim me"
repeated a hundred times over, just the way
my father would have wanted.

What made him keep this jungle,
this oasis of gnats and snakes?
Usually a practical man, was this his soft spot,
his attempt at tradition? Perhaps
this was meant as his escape, when
western mountains became too steep,
winters too harsh, his family too cold.
Maybe he identified himself in this land:
under-appreciated, deserted, stoic to the end.

I have waited five years now for the value
to change, an inkling to the decision I must make.

But the land is stubborn, a member of the family
in its own right. It will not budge before me.

Maybe it's no easier to walk away a second time.

The blue cheese dressing rattles
inside the refrigerator door, half-empty.
I thought about opening it,
drenching each red-green leaf,
just to fill my mouth
with something that you loved.

TO MY PLAGIARIST

I don't know why you'd want them:
the long, hard stares, the suspicion.
No one believes you
when you write about the dark
days when you tried to bury
your face in water. No one willingly
puts their ear to the well. I wish
I could send you the whole package:
the voices, the empty bucket,
puddles that refuse your reflection.
But none will sit still under the twine.

I don't blame you, but I'm curious.
What would make you steal
such pain?

IV

The Farmer's Almanac won't soon forget
this season: pansies overwhelmed
by the persistent fist of frost,
potholes filling the street like fresh blooms.
The year even the deer fled south
across the Mason-Dixon line. The mail
was never delivered, and a dangerous deficit
of mittens hit the economy hard.
Everything seemed as arduous
as a struggling, frozen stream,
our words brittle and bitter,
the mouth of my lover
a horizon that swallowed its sun.

Vows shape-shift like clouds
into whatever we want them to be:
forever, never, a trial.
Nothing will carry the weight
it's given. Put a collar on the cat
and she only hunkers low as fog.

Emptied of our possessions,
the house is finally clean
of argument. Moonlight slips
through the window,
white as a canine's tooth.

The click of the deadbolt
loud as a slap, the neighbors
watch me pack the car.

They do not wave good-bye.

My breasts itch
like dual ends
of a stale French loaf
crazy in their crust, a scab
that cannot heal.

I point to the culprits: *Boo-boo,*
I say to the doctor. Reverting
to child speak, I hope he can heal
like a father—a quick kiss,
a tousle of the hair, and voilá!
He stares kindly, waiting for my
denial to pass. But my thoughts,
wild and infected, flow like blood,
my words as ineffective as T cells.

Metastasis.
Perhaps not yet, but my breasts
are bombs—would I cradle a grenade?

I touch them the way many
melted men have touched them,
pass my baubles to the surgeon
like Picasso's mutilated muse,
then recede into darkness.

AN ALCHEMIST RETIRES

I do not regret my attempts
at transmutation—does not
the painter create flowers
from oil? What of magicians,
skillfully plucking hares
from the bottom of their hats?

Yet I've come to depend
on the reliability of lead:
its refusal to rise at my will,
dense as a dream, heavy as failure.

My mortar and pestle grinds
but dust, the alembic distills
the liquor of a peach.
A man knows when it is time
to take down the shingle.
I grow tired, and have yet
to create a star in my fireplace.
So little has come from these hands.

FLOOD

Water rushes along the curb,
storm sewers hush the morning
back to sleep. The snow
was just the beginning.
Now rain holds reign,
banishes the snow from streets.

Creeks and streams swallow
their tongues. The footbridge
begins to come apart, drops
its nails into the rising water
like coins, making a wish
for an afterlife. A groundhog
has a home on the bank,
but a deep slumber ignores
a flood water's roar.

Drops smack against the panes,
thousands of tiny fists. We fill bag
after bag with sand, lock the door.

We cannot sleep, always straining
for some sound, some hint that
nature, with her long, fluid fingers,
has let herself in.

ANATOMY

We did not expect a young woman,
her skin still tight, but cold.
We were afraid to touch, her features
not the kind to beckon young men:
her nose a mountain on the plain
of her face, her neck and arms
thin as dried reeds. But here,
hands sheathed in latex,
our scalpel blades disappeared

into her skin, until we pushed back
the clean lines of dermis like curtains,
her small muscles and organs revealed.
Awestruck, the Latin rose to our lips
like a sigh: the graceful length
of her gracilis, her shapely gluteus medius,
the sweep of the orbicularis oris
beneath her stiff, unsmiling lips.

We were never satisfied again

to kiss the surface of a pretty face.
At last we'd learned the secrets
of the deep, become enamored
with what lay beneath.

A SCIENTIST'S ACROSTIC

Scientists are like beetles
Crawling over the earth, antennae twitching,
In tune with the mysteries
Einstein whispered under a star-polished
Night sky. He chose the celestial playground by
Convention—even logic, as beetles know, can be
Enhanced by beauty.

Illumination dawns after years of
Scratching through dark leaves, dirt.

Lying on one's back, legs flailing,
Is temporary, and not, as some imagine
Fundamental failure or
Even such a bad thing.

Some day it will come to this.
You will refuse to get up
from the squeaky rocker
on the cabin porch, flecking paint.
Your notebook will lie
beside you and stay there.
Someone will mention calling
an ambulance, but you will insist
students gather on the dusty planks,
strain to hear your voice.
You will only have kind words
for their poems: the sunlight
death brings! Sentences will trail off
into the surrounding mountains,
many will lose their way.

You can't go on like this,
but this is what you know:
blue veins will rise to the
surface of your frail,

paper skin, curve into
words you had buried deep,
just for this occasion, the last
thub-dubs of your heart
a Morse code of rhythm and song.

Many imagine it was like a jigsaw—
but no, it was more like cataloging
a collection of rare, exotic birds:
examining how the plumage
of beryllium resembled magnesium,
the curve of the wing,
the clutch of their feet
on prey.

Mendeleev was a serious man, never
jumped from the path of a black cat.
But the ones who eluded him—
the ghosts of empty squares,
the unnamed fledglings lost
to the deep woods—
it was almost too much.

What kept him going
on those nights when rain
fell like mercury in the dark,

when the wind threatened
to blow the lantern out,
were all the ones placed correctly,
fireflies alive in the jar.

His ancestors called softly
at first, but grew in urgency
over the years, anxious to see
completed what they began—
And so thou wilt call
thunder and destruction
if thou know the art.

He knew he could find it,
how to make atoms dance
in the grand ballroom of collision,
chandelier bright—
these were the musings
burning in Oppenheimer's head
a rhythm quite clear
quick, slow, quick quick, slow
metronome for devastation,
a faint ticking to make the night
appear mysteriously high noon.

Can it be this simple?
When one war ends, another
begins. This is what he knew
best, eyes full of ash, the rising
sun eclipsed. How hollow
are the refrains of discovery
when one has become death,
destroyer of worlds.

The anchorman appears too small
for his suit, but my, he has a big, red
grin. Behind him, a map of the Middle East,
masked men sliding down a mud-slapped
street. The anchor eyes the clip,
forms his hand into a gun, and levels
with us: *bang bang bang*

The weather girl is dressed for hula.
She makes the sign for sun, swings
her hips. She sings something
unintelligible, something full of vowels,
except the part: *damn hot.* Pineapples
jut from the deep root of Florida.

It's looking like another pretty day
in paradise until a cop car
skids to a stop in front of the courthouse.
Boys pile out. *One, two, three...*
They keep coming, faces alternately

red and blue, beaming. They know
there's no need to despair. Granny's
holding a bake sale to post their bail.
She's pumping a bag of chocolate chips
high above her head—a hero, a champ.

HOW TO FIGHT OFF DESPAIR

You'll be tempted
to use your fists
but remember:
violence won't
get you anywhere

Instead, fit your soul
into the paper bag
of your voice and watch
it rise like a small
balloon. Despair
has no defense
against the weightlessness
of joy, the power of song

Allow the rhythm
of your breathing
to become a turning
point, fill the room
with your voice, let

him have it, I say,
the old songs your mama
used to sing you:
a porch light on the dark
plains where you thought
there was nothing
for miles

ANOTHER IMAGINED INFIDELITY

Sometimes I wake up
at three in the morning,
wounded: a temptress running
her fingers down your arm
at a dinner party, you in bed
with my best friend from childhood.
Every now and then, you hit
a new low. This time,
an exotic woman was lost
and called our number by mistake.
You guided her through
unfamiliar territory out of kindness,
your voice terribly calm.

We have been married too long
for this. When I rouse you
from sleep to detail your crimes,
you groggily humor me. *Why
does this one count against me?*
Because I, too, was lost once,
and you are still the landmark I cling to.

ACKNOWLEDGEMENTS

Grateful acknowledgement is made to the editors of the following periodicals, where some of these poems first appeared:

The Atlanta Review: "Body of Water," "Model of the Atom"
The Distillery: "Something in Us Loves Ruin"
Forpoetry.com: "Building the Periodic Table," "To End All Wars"
Front Range Review: "Booger"
Gecko: "Submerged"
Green Hills Literary Lantern: "Phosphorescence"
GSU Review: "A Brief History of Mathematics," "Explaining Relativity to the Cat"
The Ledge: "The Element Refugees"
New York Quarterly: "Harsh Winter," "On the Decision Not to Have Children"
Plainsongs: "Thoughts from Anesthesia"
Poet Lore: "The End of the Workshop"
Poetry Now: "How My Parents Met"
Red Rock Review: "Will This Be On The Test?"
Rhino: "Song of Shadow"
Snakeskin: "Summer of Fractions"

Several of these poems appeared in the chapbook *Explaining Relativity to the Cat* (Pudding House Press, 2004).

"Body of Water" was also selected for inclusion in *The Atlanta Review*'s 10th Anniversary special issue.

Jennifer Gresham grew up in the (near extinct) rural outskirts of Tampa, Florida. She has earned degrees in biochemistry from the U.S. Air Force Academy (B.S.), the University of Oklahoma (M.S.), and the University of Maryland (Ph.D.). Her chapbook, *Explaining Relativity to the Cat*, was published by Pudding House Press in 2004. She currently lives with her husband and their cat in Chevy Chase, Maryland.